A Look Inside Caves

Darrin Cates

Rosen Readers

Rosen Classroom™

New York

Published in 2014 by The Rosen Publishing Group, Inc.
29 East 21st Street, New York, NY 10010

Book Design: Jon D'Rozario

Photo Credits: Cover stefano spezi/Shutterstock.com; p. 5 Khoroshunova Olga/Shutterstock.com; p. 7 (ice cave) S J Francis/Shutterstock.com; p. 7 (sea cave) Alberto Loyo/Shutterstock.com; p. 9 aquatic creature/Shutterstock.com; p. 11 stocker1970/Shutterstock.com; p. 13 hangingpixels/Shutterstock.com; p. 15 Joshua Haviv/Shutterstock.com; p. 17 David Boyer/National Geographic/Getty Images; p. 19 Matt Jeppson/Shutterstock.com; p. 21 AISPIX by Image Source/ Shutterstock.com; p. 22 (notebook) EsbenOxholm/Shutterstock.com; p. 22 (background) doodle/Shutterstock.com.

ISBN: 978-1-4777-2337-1
6-pack ISBN: 978-1-4777-2338-8

Manufactured in the United States of America

CPSIA Compliance Information: Batch #CS13RC: For further information contact Rosen Publishing, New York, New York at 1-800-237-9932.

Contents

A Mysterious World

Caves are beautiful and mysterious places. However, they must be **explored** carefully. Inside caves, people can find rock **formations** and animals that can't be seen anywhere but these dark, wet places.

Millions of caves can be found below Earth's **surface**. No one knows for sure how many caves exist. Many are still waiting to be discovered and explored.

Some caves can be hundreds of miles long!

Creating a Cave

Some caves are made by the ocean's crashing waves. These are called sea caves. They're found in cliffs by the sea. The waves pound strongly against the cliffs, chipping away the rock and forming caves.

Other caves are found in huge pieces of ice, called glaciers. When the ice starts to melt, the running water forms a cave. This is called an ice cave.

Moving water can be very powerful. If it moves strongly enough, it can create sea caves and ice caves after hundreds of years.

ice cave
sea cave

Special caves are found near **volcanoes**. These caves are **created** by melted rock called lava. Lava caves form when the outside of the flowing lava cools more quickly than the center. This forms a hard crust of rock around the flowing hot lava. When the hot lava moves on, a cave is left behind. Lava caves have sharp rocks that can tear your clothes!

Lava is the melted rock that comes out of a volcano. It's very hot!

The most common type of cave is formed in rocks that can be easily broken down over time, such as limestone. Rainwater slowly goes through cracks in the rocks and mixes with a gas called carbon dioxide (KAHR-buhn dy-AHK-syd). This turns the water into an **acid**, which breaks down the rock until it forms a cave.

It takes millions of years for caves to form!

Rock Formations

Once a cave is formed, water continues to slowly drip into it from the ground above. This water eventually dries up and leaves behind minerals. A mineral is a solid, nonliving thing that's found in nature.

Over time, these minerals begin to make new rock formations in the cave. Some of these rock formations hang from the top, or roof, of the cave. These are stalactites (stuh-LAK-tyts).

Stalactites hold tightly to the top of the cave!

stalactites

A different kind of rock formation is created when water slowly drips from the roof of the cave to the floor. Then, the minerals form a shape that grows from the floor up toward the roof. This rock formation is called a stalagmite (stuh-LAG-myt).

Stalagmites and stalactites can grow together, too. This forms a column, which is a rock formation that stretches from the floor of the cave to its roof.

The rock formations in a cave get their color from the minerals that make them.

stalagmites

Sometimes, water flows over the rocks in a cave or down its walls. The minerals left behind after the water is gone create a rock formation called flowstone. This often looks like a waterfall made of rock!

Another rock formation found in caves is called a curtain. It's also formed by water running along the walls of a cave before drying and leaving minerals behind.

Some rock formations in caves have stripes that look like bacon. We call these formations cave bacon!

Cave Creatures

Caves are home to many different kinds of animals. Some only make their homes at the front of a cave, such as bears, foxes, and snakes. These animals still need light, so they can't go too far into a cave.

Other animals can't live outside the darkness of a cave. They're usually blind, and they often have colorless skin!

Animals that live in caves, such as these salamanders, are called troglobites.

Going Caving!

You can sometimes find another kind of animal in caves, too—humans! People love to explore caves. This fun activity is commonly called caving or spelunking (spih-LUNG-king). Caving must be done very carefully and always with other people. It's important to move slowly and to carry the right supplies to safely explore a cave.

When caving is done safely and correctly, it can be a lot of fun!

You can learn a lot about nature by exploring the world inside a cave!

A Caving Checklist

For light

- ✓ helmet with headlight
- ✓ flashlights
- ✓ extra batteries
- ✓ candle and matches

For clothing

- ✓ layers of clothing made of wool
- ✓ two pairs of pants
- ✓ gloves
- ✓ heavy socks
- ✓ boots

For eating and drinking

- ✓ water in a strong bottle
- ✓ food that's easy to carry (like peanuts and raisins)

Glossary

acid (AA-suhd) A liquid that can burn things and break them down.

create (kree-AYT) To make something.

explore (ihk-SPLOHR) To search something to find out more about it.

formation (fohr-MAY-shun) Shape.

surface (SUHR-fuhs) The top part of something that can be seen.

volcano (vahl-KAY-noh) An opening in Earth's surface through which hot, liquid rock sometimes flows.

Index